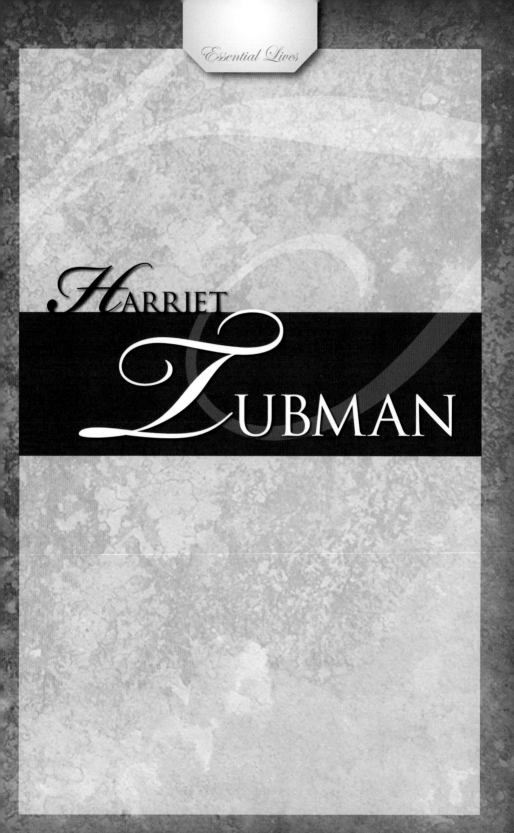

Essential Lives

HARRIET TUBMAN

Essential Lives

HARRIET ZUBMAN

BY M.J. COSSON

Content Consultant
Richard Nelson, Ph.D.
U.S. Intellectual and Cultural History

ABDO
Publishing Company

CREDITS

Published by ABDO Publishing Company, 8000 West 78th Street, Edina, Minnesota
55439. Copyright © 2008 by Abdo Consulting Group, Inc. International copyrights
reserved in all countries. No part of this book may be reproduced in any form without
written permission from the publisher. The Essential Library™ is a trademark and
logo of ABDO Publishing Company.

Printed in the United States.

Editor: Paula Lewis
Cover Design: Becky Daum
Interior Design: Lindaanne Donohoe

Library of Congress Cataloging-in-Publication Data
Cosson, M. J.

  Harriet Tubman / M.J. Cosson.
     p. cm.—(Essential lives)
  Includes bibliographical references and index.
   ISBN 978-1-59928-842-0
  1. Tubman, Harriet, 1820?-1913—Juvenile literature. 2. Slaves—United States—
Biography—Juvenile literature. 3. African American women—Biography—Juvenile
literature. 4. African Americans—Biography—Juvenile literature. 5. Underground
Railroad—Juvenile literature. I. Title.

E444.T82C67 2007
973.7'115092—dc22

  [B]
                                        2007012270

TABLE OF CONTENTS

Overseers with slaves cutting sugarcane

A Hit on the Head

Born into slavery, the adolescent girl was from the Brodess plantation near Bucktown, Maryland. Years earlier, her master had decided that she was fit for heavy outdoor labor. As was his custom, he had hired her out to work on the harvest at a nearby plantation. Although she was small, the girl had been working at hard labor for many years. She was strong.

As the girl worked, one of the other slaves ran past her in the fields. She looked up in time to watch the overseer take off after the slave. It is not clear if the girl was ordered to chase the slave, whether she ran along to see what would happen, or whether she was trying to help the slave escape. Whatever the reason, the young slave girl followed.

The runaway slave ran into a small country general store in Bucktown. The overseer ran in, and the girl followed. The runaway slave ran back out the door while the girl was in the doorway. Again, it is unclear whether she was trying to help the runaway escape or whether she was caught in the doorway by mistake.

The overseer picked up a two-pound (.9 kg) lead weight from a shelf and hurled it through the door after the runaway slave. It missed the runaway. Instead, it hit the girl in the forehead.

The lead weight smashed into the girl's forehead with such force that it fractured her skull. It also tore off a piece of her shawl and rammed the cloth inside her forehead. She fell to the ground senseless. Bleeding and fainting, she was carried back to the plantation. She had no bed, so she was laid on the seat of a loom. She remained there until the next day, drifting in and out of consciousness. A weaker person might have died, but this young girl survived. Soon after, although her head was still aching and bleeding, she was forced to return to work in the fields.

With a huge, bloody dent in her forehead and a dazed expression, she tried to work but fainted often. When she began falling down and passing out in the fields, the overseer sent the girl back to her owner. He also sent Mr. Brodess a report stating that she was "not worth a sixpence."[1]

In time, her head

Plantation Economy

Many areas in the South were ideal for agriculture. Early European settlers found that cash crops paid the greatest return for the effort required. Crops included tobacco, rice, sugarcane, and hemp. With the invention of the cotton gin in 1793, cotton became the most important crop.

Large-scale plantations required many workers. The most cost-effective labor was slave labor imported from Africa beginning in the early 1700s. Slave trade was banned in 1808, but a slave owner also owned any children born to his or her slaves.

Slaves were used not only for field labor but also as cooks, maids, and other servants in the big plantation house. Some owners hired out their slaves to their neighbors and kept the money the slaves earned.

Slaves were treated as property and in any way the owner saw fit. If a slave misbehaved or tried to run away, the master could punish them. Whippings and beatings were typical. The only thing slaves could do was buy their freedom or run away. Most slaves did not have the means to buy their freedom, so running north was the only way out of slavery. If a slave was caught, the punishment was severe.

wound healed, although it left a permanent dent in her forehead. One eyelid drooped slightly. The scar, and other effects of the injury, gave her a vacant, hollow-eyed stare that strangers mistook for stupidity. In later years, the girl would learn to use this look to her advantage.

The girl suffered from terrible headaches. But the worst effect of the skull fracture was not the pain—it was that the slave girl would fall asleep suddenly. Sometimes she even fell asleep in the middle of a sentence. Then after a period of time, she would awake and continue talking, unaware that she had been sleeping. This continued through her long and adventurous life.

This young slave girl was small and illiterate. Because she could not read, she did not know geography and she could not use a map. If she received a message in writing, someone had to read it to her. If she wanted to send a letter, someone had to write it for her. She did not speak proper English.

This young girl, Araminta Ross, was born into slavery in the 1820s. How could such a girl escape to freedom? How could she lead others to freedom time and time again? How could she become a scout, a spy, and a nurse in the Civil War? How could she speak for the cause of freedom in front of hundreds of people,

The Missouri Compromise

In 1820, there were 22 states in the United States. Half were free states and half were slave states. At that time, the balance of power in the Senate between the North and South was preserved. Congress admitted Missouri to the Union as a slave state, while Maine was admitted as a free state. The balance of power in the Senate continued, but the North had more power in the House of Representatives.

The territory of the Louisiana Purchase was divided along the southern border of Missouri so that the southern part was slave and the northern part was free. Only those states south of that line, and Missouri, would be slave states. The U.S. Supreme Court's Dred Scott decision in 1857 declared the Missouri Compromise unconstitutional because it permitted Congress to prohibit slavery in some places. The states did not agree on the issue of slavery—neither did the U.S. Congress and Supreme Court.

including government officials and wealthy whites? How could she start a home for the aged? How could she become Harriet Tubman, one of our nation's bravest heroes? ⌐

U.S. Map Following Missouri Compromise 1820

- Free States and Territories
- Slave States and Territories
- Closed to slavery by the Missouri Compromise
- Open to slavery by the Missouri Compromise
- Spanish Possession
- ⭐ Washington D.C.
- - - - Missouri Compromise Line

In 1820, the United States was divided between free states and slave states.

TO BE SOLD on board the
Ship *Bance-Island*, on tuesday the 6th
of *May* next, at *Ashley-Ferry*, a choice
cargo of about 250 fine healthy
NEGROES,
just arrived from the
Windward & Rice Coast.
—The utmost care has
already been taken, and
shall be continued, to keep them free from
the least danger of being infected with the
SMALL-POX, no boat having been on
board, and all other communication with
people from *Charles-Town* prevented.
Austin, Laurens, & Appleby.

N. B. Full one Half of the above Negroes have had the
SMALL-POX in their own Country.

Newspaper advertisement announcing the arrival of Africans to be sold as slaves

GROWING UP AS A SLAVE

The first African slaves were brought to North
America in 1619. Slavery was an economic
boon for plantation owners, especially in the South
with its farming economy. Plantation owners bought
slaves on the auction block, and the children of slaves

became slaves too. Slave owners had a ready-made labor force. They did not have to pay wages—they only had to provide the bare necessities of food, clothing, and shelter. The field workers had Sunday off. They often used that day to hunt, fish, or trap to supplement the small amounts of food their masters provided. Slaves often grew vegetables in their own garden patches.

Owners used their slaves for various types of work. Their favorite or best-behaved slaves worked in the home as servants, cooks, or washerwomen. Most slaves worked in the fields picking crops. Tobacco and cotton were major crops in the South. Some slaves were miners; others tended livestock or were boatmen. By law, slaves could not be educated in schools. So, if a job could be done without reading, writing, or math, a slave might be doing it.

A Maryland law dating back to 1712 stated that a slave child's fate followed that of his or her mother's. If the mother was a slave, the child was born a slave, even if the child's father was a free man.

There are no records, but around 1790, the slave named "Rit" (short for Harriet) Green was born. Her mother, Modesty, had come to

Thousands of Slaves

In 1790, there were almost 700,000 slaves in the United States. Most of the slaves worked in agriculture.

An artist's interpretation of the deck of a slave ship packed tightly with slaves

the United States on a slave ship.

When Rit was old enough, she "jumped the broom" with the slave Ben Ross. There was no legal marriage ceremony for slaves, but they had their own ceremony from the Ashanti tradition in Africa. The couple held hands and jumped backwards over a broom in front of their friends and relatives. After each successful jump, the broom was held higher. Whoever stumbled first was forced to heed the wishes of the other in marriage. In the case of Rit and Ben, it is unknown who stumbled first, but we do know that they had a long married life, and together they raised a large family.

One of their children was Araminta "Minty" Ross. Because her mother and her grandmother had been slaves, Minty was born into slavery. No official records were kept about a slave's birth, so her exact date of birth is unknown. At various times later in her life, she gave her date of birth as 1820 or 1825.

Araminta Ross was probably born on the Brodess plantation. Her master was not a rich plantation owner. To earn money, he hired his slaves out to nearby plantations. When Minty was very young, she was allowed to run free. She wore a dress similar to a cloth flour sack with holes cut out for her head and arms. This is the only clothing she wore, even during the winter. She did not have a comb for her hair, so it stuck out from her head. Minty's wild freedom lasted until she was about five years old. Then she was put to work.

In later years, she recalled that a woman called Miss Susan drove up to her master's plantation and asked for a young girl to help care for her baby. Miss Susan would only pay very low wages, so the master sent little Minty. By day, Minty's job was a maid. By night, she made sure the baby stayed quiet while Miss Susan slept.

Miss Susan had a temper. Once, she asked Minty to dust. Minty dusted with a rag, and the dust settled right back down on the furniture. Miss Susan whipped her. Minty dusted again, and the dust settled back down.

Miss Susan whipped her again. At last, Miss Susan's sister, Miss Emily, showed Minty how to dust properly.

Minty was so small that she had to sit on the floor to hold Miss Susan's baby. At night, she sat on the floor between Miss Susan's bed and the baby's cradle. Miss Susan kept a whip on a shelf by her bed. If her baby cried during the night, she grabbed the whip and used it on Minty. Not allowed

Nat Turner's Rebellion

Nat Turner was born a slave in 1800. He was intelligent and deeply religious. As an adult, he had several visions that he took as signs to rise up and rebel against his master. In 1831, Nat Turner led a rebellion in Southhampton County, Virginia—less than 100 miles (160 km) from the Brodess Plantation where Araminta lived. Nat Turner and more than 40 other slaves rebelled against their masters. The slaves killed nearly 60 white people.

Turner escaped and eluded his captors for several weeks. When he was caught, he was tried and hanged. Another 55 slaves were also executed.

Slaveholders and mobs became hysterical and afraid of another such uprising. As many as 200 black people were killed as a result of Nat Turner's rebellion. Many were innocent people. Because of the rebellion, the Virginia State Legislature considered abolishing slavery, but slavery was kept by a close vote. The rebellion fueled the growing distrust between slaves and slaveholders.

to sleep, Minty eventually became sick and was returned to the Brodess plantation.

Araminta was hired out again and again. When the work was done or if she became sick, Minty was always sent back to her parents on the master's plantation. When she was six years old, she was sent away to learn weaving. She was soon sent back.

Araminta recalled working in one house when the master and mistress got into an argument in the kitchen. Minty was standing beside the sugar bowl. She had never tasted sugar before. While the couple was distracted in their argument, she popped a cube of sugar in her mouth. The mistress saw Minty take the sugar and chased her. Minty hid in the pigpen for a few days. She ate what the pigs ate. The mother pig was protective of the food—Minty had to scramble to get anything to eat. At last she realized that she could not continue to live with the pigs, so she gave herself up to whippings and was promptly sent home.

Realizing Araminta was not fit for domestic work, she was hired out for heavy labor. She plowed fields or lifted barrels of flour, lumber, and other heavy items. She even worked when she had the measles until she became very sick. Again, she was sent home.

When Minty was not hired out, she hunted, fished,

and trapped with her father. She learned about plants and roots for food and medicine. These experiences helped Araminta learn how to survive in the wild. Her work in the fields, lifting and pulling alongside men twice her size, gave her strength, power, and endurance. These traits served Araminta Ross well in her later life.

> "I grew up like a neglected weed—ignorant of liberty, having no experience of it." [1]
> —Harriet Tubman

Slaves picking cotton

An escaped slave captured under the Fugitive Slave Act

A Taste of Freedom

Araminta continued her life in the fields
and forests, going where her master
sent her and doing the work that needed to be done.
At one point she was hired out to a man named John
Stewart, who allowed his slaves to hire their time.

If a slave wanted to hire out in his or her spare time to another master for pay, the slave could do so, as long as part of the pay went to the master. Araminta did this and split the money with Stewart.

Araminta's father, Ben Ross, had been promised that he would be emancipated when he turned 45. In 1840, he was granted his freedom. His wife, Rit, however, was still a slave. Because a slave's fate followed that of the mother's, Araminta and all of Ben and Rit's children were still slaves.

In 1844, Araminta "jumped the broom" with John Tubman. Just as birth records were not kept, marriage records of African Americans—slave or free—were not kept either. John Tubman was a free black man. It is not known whether he was born free or whether he became free as an adult. It was very unusual, however, for a free man to marry a slave woman because his children would be slaves too.

About the time that Araminta married John Tubman and changed her last name, she also changed her first name to Harriet. She had always been close to her parents, and the

Runaways and Fugitives

There was a difference between a runaway and a fugitive. Many slaves ran away to escape punishment. They either were returned to face their punishment or they came back on their own. Only runaways who sought permanent freedom were considered fugitives.

name change might have been a sign of affection for her mother. Or it might be that Araminta looked like her mother and so people called her Harriet. Perhaps this was a step in striking out for her freedom. For whatever reason, from about 1844 on, Araminta Ross became Harriet Tubman.

Around the time that Harriet wed John Tubman, she paid a lawyer five dollars to investigate her slave status. The lawyer found that the owner's will allowed for Rit to become free when she reached the age of 45. That meant her children should also be given their freedom when they reached 45. Harriet had 20 to 25 more years of slavery ahead of her. However, the promise to Harriet's mother in the will was broken. Rit was kept a slave ten years longer than she should have been.

From 1847 to 1849, Harriet lived and worked on the property of Dr. Anthony Thompson. In 1849, her master, Mr. Brodess, died. This meant Harriet and two of her brothers were to be sold. It is unclear whether they were to be sold to a chain gang or to a distant plantation. Harriet had seen two of her sisters sold off to a chain gang, and she vowed to run away if that should happen to her.

> *I had reasoned this out in my mind; there was one of two things I had a right to—liberty or death. If I could not have*

Quakers during a worship service

one, I would have the other, for no man should take me
alive. I should fight for my liberty as long as my strength
lasted.[1]

ESCAPE TO FREEDOM

In September 1849, Harriet's escape to freedom
started out with her brothers, but they quickly turned
back. Harriet continued by herself. She carried a quilt
that she had pieced together and was very proud of.
Along the way, she asked for the help of a white woman,
probably because someone had told her that the woman
could help her. The woman might have been a Quaker.

Quakers

Quakers are members of a Christian religious organization called the Society of Friends. They believe that all people are created equal, and they oppose war and slavery. In 1775, they founded the first anti-slavery group in the colonies. They believed that slavery was morally wrong. The Quakers supported the abolition of slavery and participated in the Underground Railroad.

Quakers were known to be against slavery. Harriet gave the quilt to the woman. In return, the woman handed her a paper with two names on it and directions to get to the first house.

When Harriet arrived at the house, she met a Quaker woman, probably Hannah Leverton. The woman handed Harriet a broom and told her to sweep the yard so that she would not be noticed. Harriet swept. That night, Harriet was helped into a covered wagon that took her to another destination. Somehow, Harriet was able to use the information on that piece of paper even though she could not read.

Harriet traveled by night and rested during the day. There was no safe way for a fugitive slave to travel, but walking north along roads in broad daylight was out of the question. Patrollers, called "paddyrollers" by the slaves, were always on the lookout for runaway slaves. Free blacks needed to carry a pass to prove that they were free. This is one reason why it was against the law to educate blacks. If they could read and write, they could forge their freedom passes.

FIFTY DOLLARS REWARD.

Ran away from Mount Welby, Prince George's County, Maryland, on Monday, the 2d inst., a negro man calling himself Joe Bond, about 25 years of age, about 5 feet 6 inches in height, stout built, copper complexion; the only mark recollected is a peculiar speck in one of his eyes. Had on when he went away a frock tweed coat, dark brown, and cap near the same color. I will give twenty-five dollars if taken in Prince George's County, Md., or in Alexandria County, Virginia; and fifty dollars if taken elsewhere and returned to me, or secured so that I get him again.

T. R. EDEL...

Piscataway, Prince George's, December 5. 1850.

Rewards were offered for fugitive slaves.

A notice in the October 3, 1849, *Cambridge Democrat* read, "MINTY, aged about 27 years, is of a chestnut color, fine looking, and [a]bout 5 feet high."[2] The notice also stated that the slave Minty had run away on September 17. A reward of $50 was offered if she was caught in Maryland. The reward jumped to $100 if she was caught out of state. The notice was signed by Eliza Ann Brodess, the daughter of Harriet's old master.

Some accounts say that abolitionists passed Harriet from house to house on her way to freedom. Other accounts say that she traveled alone, following rivers and using the North Star as her guide. There is reason to believe that she did both.

Late in 1849, Harriet arrived in Philadelphia, Pennsylvania, unharmed. For the first time in her life, she was free. She said that when she crossed the Pennsylvania border to reach freedom,

> *I looked at my hands to see if I was the same person now I was free. There was such a glory over everything. The sun came like gold through the trees and over the fields, and I felt like I was in heaven.*[3]

The feeling did not last, however. Harriet knew that she was alone, and that the rest of her family was still in bondage.

> *I had crossed the line of which I had so long been dreaming. I was free, but there was no one to welcome me to the land of freedom. I was a stranger in a strange land, and my home after all was down in the old cabin quarter, with the old folks and my brothers and sisters. But to this solemn resolution I came: I was free and they should be free also; I would make a home for them in the North...*[4]

CROSSING THE LINE—AGAIN

In Philadelphia, Harriet began work as a cook. She saved as much money as she could because she had a goal to bring her family to freedom too. Within a year of her escape, Harriet established contact with her family back home.

One of Harriet's sisters who had been sold had a daughter named Kizzy. John Bowley, Kizzy's husband, was a free black. In 1850, he contacted Harriet in Philadelphia. She learned that Kizzy and her two children were to be sold off from the Brodess plantation. Bowley asked for Harriet's advice, and she helped him plan how to free them. Harriet sent word she would be waiting when they got across the bay.

For Harriet, returning to Maryland meant crossing over the line of freedom to a slave state. Bravely, Harriet went to Baltimore, Maryland, and found a safe house for Kizzy and her children.

In December of 1850, Kizzy and her children were at the slave auction site in front of the county courthouse in Cambridge, Maryland. Legend has it that Bowley bid for Kizzy and the children, but when it was time to pay for them, he did not have the money. The auctioneer left Kizzy and the children and went to dinner. He may have thought that a young slave woman with two young children could not get very far in the middle of a crowd. He was wrong. Bowley managed to get Kizzy and the children away from the auction site and onto a boat. He rowed them across the bay to where Harriet was waiting for them. She kept Kizzy and the children safely hidden until she could smuggle them north to freedom.

The Fugitive Slave Act of 1850

In 1842, the Supreme Court had ruled that states did not have to aid in the return of runaway slaves. Then, Congress passed the Compromise of 1850 in an attempt to appease southern states. The compromise revised the Fugitive Slave Act. The law now gave slave owners "the right to organize a posse at any point in the United States to aid in recapturing runaway slaves. Courts and police everywhere in the United States were obligated to assist them..."[5]

Private citizens also had an obligation to assist in the recapture of runaways. People who were caught helping slaves had to serve jail time and pay fines. Enforcement of the Fugitive Slave Act caused many northern blacks to flee to Canada. Approximately 3,000 African Americans crossed the border into Canada within 90 days of the enactment of the Fugitive Slave Act.

In the spring of 1851, Harriet returned again to rescue her brother Moses and two other men. She was able to lead them to freedom. In late 1851, she went south a third time to rescue her husband, John, even though he was already a free man. John Tubman had not come north to join Harriet since she had escaped, so she went south to get

South Carolina slaves who were hired out were required to wear a slave tag.

him. It would have been dangerous for him to go north with Harriet because if he was caught with her, he could have lost his freedom.

Harriet wanted to bring John back with her, but he refused to leave. He reminded her that he was already

The Latimer Law

Massachusetts state officials could not aid in the capture of slaves or use state facilities to hold them. Ohio, Connecticut, Vermont, Rhode Island, and Pennsylvania adopted similar laws. The Fugitive Slave Act of 1850 voided all state laws, and federal agents were given authority over the states. The agents could even give a verdict without a trial by jury.

free. In her absence, he had taken a new wife who was a free woman. Her husband's rejection was difficult, but it only made her work harder. Later, she said that she "dropped him out of [her] heart."[6]

In December of 1851, Harriet Tubman made a new commitment. Her journey south would not be wasted. Previously she had gone to get family and friends. This time, she collected a party of fugitives and brought them safely to Philadelphia. Harriet Tubman had committed herself to a new cause: the Underground Railroad. ⌐

Fugitive slaves escaped using tunnels such as this four- by five-foot (1- by 1.5-m) tunnel under a home in Wilton, Connecticut.

Slaves heading for freedom

The Underground Railroad

What was the Underground Railroad? Where did it start, and where did it go? The name may have originated around 1831 when a fugitive slave slipped out of his master's sight. The slave owner had been hunting his runaway slave but came home empty handed. He remarked that the slave disappeared so suddenly that he must have taken an underground railroad.

The Underground Railroad began at about the time the railroads were being built across the United States. While escaping slaves traveled primarily by foot or wagon, railroad terms became part of the Underground Railroad. Places provided for fugitive slaves to stay were called stations or depots. Business or property owners who housed the fugitives were the stationmasters. Because of the potential danger, stationmasters did not give out their names. Tubman became a conductor of the Underground Railroad. She traveled with her passengers and brought them to freedom in the North.

But, when Tubman became a conductor on the Underground Railroad, did she really know what she was getting into? Tubman was illiterate; she only knew what she was told. However, she was able to determine the good from the bad, the necessary from the unnecessary.

Abolitionists in Philadelphia

The Free African Society was founded in 1787. In 1787, Benjamin Franklin was the first president of the Pennsylvania Society for the Promotion of the Abolition of Slavery. A black man named Robert Purvis was president from 1845–1850.

In 1850 when Tubman reached Philadelphia, abolition lectures and debates were hosted by African Americans. Tubman learned that she was not alone in the quest for freedom.

She possessed a strong desire for freedom for all people born into bondage. Tubman wanted to see slavery abolished, and she worked to that end. The Underground Railroad was made up of people doing what they could.

PEOPLE HELPING PEOPLE

Fugitive slaves might be put up in someone's shed or cellar, be given food and medicine, and still never know who was helping them. Quakers had strong beliefs against slavery and were organized to help escaping slaves. Stationmasters were often free blacks.

Most slaves had to escape on their own. It was risky for

Sojourner Truth

Isabella Baumfree was born a slave in Ulster County, New York, around 1797. As a slave almost six feet (1.8 m) tall, she performed heavy-duty labor for her master. When her master refused to free her, she declared herself free in 1826. She then began to travel the country preaching. She could not read, but she always said she could read people. In 1843, she renamed herself Sojourner Truth. As a Quaker, she knew many abolitionists and supported President Lincoln and the Union Army.

Known as a powerful speaker, the following quote is a portion of her famous "Ain't I a Woman?" speech. It was presented in 1851, at the Women's Rights Convention in Ohio.

"That man over there says that women need to be helped into carriages, and lifted over ditches, and to have the best place everywhere. Nobody ever helps me into carriages, or over mud-puddles, or gives me any best place! And ain't I a woman? Look at me! Look at my arm! I have ploughed and planted, and gathered into barns, and no man could head me! And ain't I a woman?"[1]

a conductor to come onto a
plantation and rally the slaves to run
away. It was risky to even meet the
fugitives, but over time, certain routes
and safe places were established.
Fugitives moved at night, traveling
between 10 and 20 miles (16 and 32
km). When they arrived at a safe place,
they would rest during the day while a
message was sent to the next station that a group of
fugitives would soon arrive.

Uncle Tom's Cabin

Harriet Beecher Stowe's *Uncle Tom's Cabin* was published in 1852. The book created an antislavery outcry.

If fugitives had forged papers indicating that they
were free, they might travel as passengers by railroad
or boat. In that case, they wore nicer clothing to pass
as free blacks. Papers were not needed in order to ride
in the cargo cars, which many did—under very poor
conditions. When a fugitive arrived in a northern city,
a place to stay, warm clothing, shoes, and a few
necessities were needed. This cost money; Tubman
became adept at raising funds.

Tubman made many contacts during her time in the
Underground Railroad, including William Still, the
Philadelphia stationmaster. He had been born a free
black in 1821 near Medford, New Jersey. Tubman and
Still worked together on many escapes.

A group of slaves escaping in the night

Thomas Garrett joined the Pennsylvania Society for the Promotion of the Abolition of Slavery in 1818. In 1822, he moved to Wilmington, Delaware, and opened a blacksmith shop and hardware store. He worked those by day. At night, he smuggled slaves to freedom. Tubman met Garrett in 1851 or 1852.

One time, Tubman's group of fugitives had to cross a bridge in Wilmington, Delaware. She knew the police were in the area looking for them. She hid her people and contacted Garrett. He found a group of black bricklayers who rode over the bridge every day with their bricks and tools. They hid Tubman and her fugitives in the bottom of their carts. As the bricklayers went home after a long day's work, the police let them pass without a search of

"If you are tired, keep going; if you are scared, keep going; if you are hungry, keep going; if you want to taste freedom, keep going."[2]

—Harriet Tubman

their carts. After all, they passed that way each and every day. No one noticed that their carts seemed to hold a few more bricks than usual.

For one of Tubman's endeavors, she asked Garrett for money. She explained that she needed shoes and passage for herself and another woman to Philadelphia. She also requested money to go to Maryland to transport a woman and her three children to safety. Tubman had paid her last cent to a driver and had no money to carry on her work. She asked Garrett for $23. Strangely, a Scotsman had just left five pounds—about $24—with Garrett. The Scotsman had told him to give it to Harriet Tubman.

Although many conductors and stationmasters on the Underground Railroad wanted anonymity for safety reasons, a few stationmasters kept records. Garrett kept accounts from the mid-1840s to the Civil War. During that time, he helped more than 2,500 slaves escape to the North. Frederick Douglass also kept count. He estimated 400 slaves passed through his house before the Civil War began.

A successful conductor in the Underground Railroad, Tubman was the only slave woman to achieve status in the Underground Railroad. She was black, female, and a fugitive—yet she repeatedly risked being a participant in the Underground Railroad. Years later, in 1904, Susan B. Anthony introduced Harriet Tubman as a living legend at the 28th Annual Convention of the New York State Women's Suffrage Association. Tubman stood up to speak. She was a small woman, and by this time, quite old. In a brave voice, she said,

> *I was conductor of the Underground Railroad for eight years, and I can say what most conductors can't say—I never ran my train off the track and I never lost a passenger.*[3]

*Susan B. Anthony and Elizabeth Cady Stanton were
involved in gaining the vote for American women.*

Harriet Tubman (left) with her family in St. Catherines, Ontario

Together and Free!

After the Fugitive Slave Act became law, citizens in the North were obliged to help recapture fugitive slaves. It was no longer safe for escaped slaves to stay in the North. Tubman said, "I wouldn't trust Uncle Sam with my people no longer, but I brought 'em clear off to Canada."[1] She made her first border crossing in 1851 and took up residence in St. Catherines in Ontario, Canada.

The winter of 1851–1852 was bitterly cold. It was Tubman's first winter in Canada, and she was not accustomed to such cold, but she put on extra layers and learned to adapt. From 1852 on, Tubman made at least one trip a year for the Underground Railroad. Sometimes she would make extra trips to rescue family or friends. She preferred going at the end of the year when nights were long and dark. She would stay in Canada for the rest of the winter. In the spring, she would travel into the States to work as a laundress or cook to earn money for her next end-of-the-year trip. While in the States, Tubman would also connect with people from the Underground Railroad in order to obtain donations for her trips.

Because of the danger, Tubman rarely went on the plantations to collect her passengers. Rather, she sent word ahead to meet at a certain place. Sometimes she would provide false information as a precaution.

Canada

After 1790, slavery was not allowed in Canada, so most escaped slaves continued on to Canada to ensure their freedom. Even so, the number of blacks in Canada never exceeded 1 percent of the population.

Then, when she felt she could trust people, she set a time and place to meet. She often met her passengers in cemeteries, where it was common to see groups of mourners gathered around a grave. Slaves who worked the fields generally had Sundays off, so Tubman planned for them to meet her on Saturday night. That way, their masters might not realize the slaves were missing until Monday morning. By the time the master could get a poster printed or a notice placed in the paper, the slaves were well on their way to freedom.

Tubman kept no records, but it is believed that most of her work involved helping slaves from Maryland and Virginia. These were areas she knew well. She might have stayed with Quakers in their meeting house or in the homes of free blacks.

Schemes and Disguises

Tubman was described as an actress who used many schemes and disguises. She even used the actual railway as part of her plan. She was confident that no one would suspect a black woman traveling on public transportation heading south. Sometimes she dressed like an old person and carried a book or newspaper. She thought anyone who saw her with reading material, traveling south, would assume she was free.

In Pennyslvania in 1696, the Quakers gave their first official declaration for the abolition of slavery.

On one trip, Tubman passed through a town near her old home. She wore a large sunbonnet to cover her face and carried two live chickens. As she passed a

This Wilton, Connecticut, home was one of the Underground Railroad depots. A door in the floor opened to a tunnel slaves used to continue their flight to freedom.

former master on the street, she let the chickens go. She avoided coming face-to-face with her old master by creating a commotion to catch her chickens.

Often, Tubman did not need a disguise. One friend said, "she seems to have command over her face and can banish all expression from her features, and look so stupid that nobody would suspect her of knowing enough to be dangerous."[2] Another friend described Tubman as "one of the most ordinary looking of her race, unlettered, no idea of geography, asleep half of the time."[3] Who would suspect Harriet Tubman of engineering the escape of so many slaves?

Unable to read, Tubman relied on pictures to recognize and make contacts with members of the Underground Railroad. She kept a stack of small visiting card portraits. Tubman could not tell strangers her plans, and she had to know the Underground Railroad people with whom she would work. When Tubman met new people in the Underground Railroad, she would show them the portrait cards. By asking the new person to identify the people on the cards, she could determine if the new person was safe.

Tubman usually took at least ten slaves at a time, kept to the back roads, and never traveled during the day. By the winter of 1853-1854, she had made at least five trips back to Maryland and saved about 30 slaves.

A CHRISTMAS GATHERING

Tubman learned her three brothers (William Henry, Benjamin, and Robert) were to be sold after Christmas Day 1854. Unable to write, someone wrote a letter for her and signed it with the name of Jacob Jackson's adopted son. The letter was sent to Jacob Jackson, a free black. Tubman hoped that Jackson would get word

to her brothers that she would come for them. The
letter said,

> Read my letter to the old folks, and give my love to them, and
> tell my brothers to be always watching unto prayer, and
> when the good old ship of Zion comes along, to be ready to
> step aboard.[4]

Postal authorities opened the letter and read it to
Jackson. He understood the letter's message and its
potential danger. However, he said he had no idea
what the letter was about. The authorities let the
matter drop. Jackson got word to Tubman's brothers
that they were to meet Harriet on Christmas Day at
their parents' cabin.

It was a custom for Ben and Rit's children to gather
at their parents' cabin on Christmas Day. But on this
Christmas Day, the three brothers met Harriet in the
shed attached to their parents' cabin. They could peer
though holes in the walls at their mother, who was
fixing Christmas dinner and waiting for her sons to
come home. They did not dare let their mother know
they were there. They feared that an emotional outburst
from her might give them away.

Tubman had not seen her parents for five years. A
friend of one of the brothers was sent into the cabin to

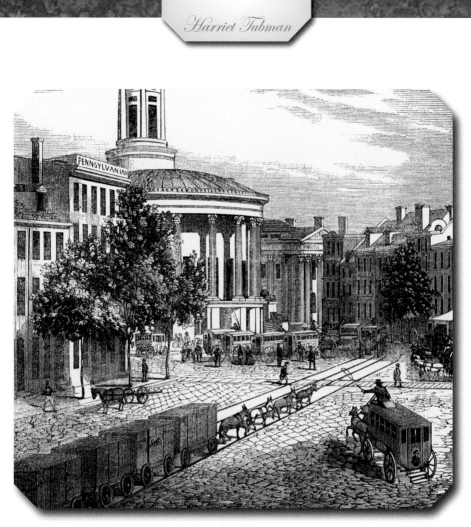

*Philadelphia in the mid-1800s was a resting place
for some of Tubman's fugitives.*

tell their father that his children were hiding in the
shed. Once Ben was outside, he was blindfolded so that
he could truthfully say that he had not seen any of
them. Tubman and her brothers left after nightfall.
Their father walked blindfolded part of the way with
them. Tubman and her brothers continued on to

Wilmington, Delaware, approximately 85 miles (136 km) north. Five days later, they were in Philadelphia, where they were given fresh clothing and food. After a day's rest, they were each given three dollars and sent by railroad to Albany, New York, and on to St. Catherines, Canada.

A FAMILY REUNION

Ben Ross had been free since 1840, and by 1855 Rit Ross was also free. But, they were under suspicion because so many slaves that they knew had escaped. They had become part of the Underground Railroad. By now, most of their family were in Canada. They wanted to be with their children and grandchildren.

In 1857, three years after the Christmas Day escape, Tubman rescued her parents. Because her parents could not walk far, she came up with a plan to make a buggy from a pair of wheels and an axle. A board became the passenger's seat. Another board hung by ropes for their feet. Tubman and her parents made the journey to Wilmington, Delaware. Garrett met them in Wilmington and provided money for the railroad trip to Canada.

With all of the family in Canada, they changed their last name from Ross to Stewart. Ben and Rit once again

The site of Harriet Tubman's house in Auburn, New York

were with their children. They were also reunited with their granddaughter Kizzy Bowley and met new family members—grandsons who had been born in Canada.

Around 1858, Senator William H. Seward offered to sell Tubman a small house on South Street in Auburn, New York. The town had a large Underground Railroad circle, and it was a good, safe place for slaves.

Ben and Rit relocated there. Now that they were both free, they could live in the United States without threat of being returned as slaves.

In 1858, Tubman journeyed to Maryland and returned with an eight-year-old black girl. The girl later told people that she was the daughter of one of Tubman's brothers. Tubman raised the girl, known as Margaret Tubman or Margaret Stewart, as her own daughter.

Tubman did not have the luxury of owning freedom papers, but she was not worried. Although there was a large price on her head, she seemed to be safe. She stayed in the United States, working and earning money to finance her next trip south.

Tubman had become known by the name "Moses." In the Bible, Moses led his people out of Egypt to freedom. Likewise, Tubman led her people north to freedom.

Harriet Tubman, the Moses of her people

The North Star helped guide Harriet Tubman as she led others to freedom.

NOT AFRAID OF DANGER

I t is possible that even with all of her trips, Tubman still followed the North Star as a guide. On cloudy nights, she knew to feel for moss on a tree trunk to tell which way was north. Tubman could follow the rivers and streams. She knew how to survive in the wild, and she did not seem to be afraid of anything. She said many times that, "When danger is near, it appears like my heart goes flutter, flutter."[1] She could sense danger. Although she might fall asleep in the middle of a sentence, she managed to lead many people to freedom.

Tubman was a master storyteller. Years later, she shared her stories. For example, one night, she and two men were moving carefully along the road when they came to an unfamiliar river. The men were afraid of crossing the river, so they sat beside the river all night. At last, it was getting light out. Tubman could not wait any longer. She walked into the river and waded across. The men, seeing that she crossed safely, followed her.

This is an unusual story for Tubman. Usually, she permitted no whimpering and threatened to kill anyone who faltered. She carried a pistol and demanded that her directions be followed.

On one trip, a man told her that he had changed his mind. He wanted to return to the plantation. Tubman could not let him leave. She knew his master would force him to tell the location of the group. When he refused to move, Tubman took out her gun, held it to his head and said, "Move or die."[2] The man went on; Tubman led him and the others to freedom.

On other trips, Tubman also led groups that included young children. She usually gave small children something to help them sleep. The fugitives could not risk being caught because of a child's cry. At times, Tubman would leave the group to scout ahead. Once, she knocked on the door of what she recalled as a station of the Underground Railroad. However, she quickly learned that the house was occupied by new residents. The previous tenants had been arrested for helping slaves flee. It was getting light out, and the fugitives needed a place to hide. The group hid quietly all day, afraid to move and afraid that bounty hunters would find them. Late in the day, a man wearing Quaker clothes passed by. Tubman heard him mutter that his wagon stood ready nearby. Her group stayed by the swamp until night, then found the wagon and continued on their journey.

Dred Scott

Dred and Harriet Scott were slaves who sued their owner in 1846 for their freedom. They had moved north with their master and lived in free territory for nine years. A series of lawsuits continued another ten years.

In 1857, the U.S. Supreme Court ruled that the Scotts had no right to sue because they were slaves. Slaves were property and so could not be citizens, and only citizens could bring lawsuits. The U.S. Supreme Court protected slavery under the U.S. Constitution.

Americans, especially in the North, reacted strongly to the Dred Scott decision. The decision played a major part in the election of Abraham Lincoln as president, which hastened the beginning of the Civil War.

John Brown

JOHN BROWN AND HARPERS FERRY

In April of 1858, Tubman met the abolitionist John Brown. He was traveling around to gain support for his plan to overthrow the government and free all slaves. He was looking for recruits. Brown spent several weeks talking with Frederick Douglass about his plans for Harpers Ferry, Virginia. He also recruited others, visiting such people as William Still in Philadelphia.

Frederick Douglass

Brown even traveled to St. Catherines in Canada
to recruit Tubman, who by now had become an
Underground Railroad hero. She had begun speaking
about her exploits to raise funds for the Underground

Railroad and to gather support against the issue of slavery. Brown was seeking Tubman's expertise. They shared a hatred of slavery.

Brown held a secret convention in Canada West on May 8, 1858. He proclaimed a new government based on a constitution he had drafted at Douglass's home. As many as 46 people attended Brown's meeting, but Tubman and Douglass did not.

On July 4, 1859, Tubman spoke in Framingham, Massachusetts. A plate was passed for Brown's cause and $40 was raised. Tubman spoke again in August in Boston under the pseudonym Harriet Garrison. By this time, she used pseudonyms to keep bounty hunters from finding her.

On August 19, 1859, Brown met with Douglass again, but Douglass had cooled on the rebellion. Tubman was in Massachusetts. By October, she was bedridden and suffering from an illness associated with her old head injury. Brown moved ahead with his plans.

Frederick Douglass (1818–1895)

Frederick Douglass was born to a slave mother who died when he was seven years old. Douglass was a brilliant speaker and one of the leaders of the abolitionist movement. Douglass toured and lectured for the American Anti-Slavery Society. In 1847 he began publishing an antislavery paper, *The North Star*.

Douglass became an advisor to President Lincoln during the Civil War. He later fought for the adoption of amendments to the U.S. Constitution that guaranteed voting rights and other civil liberties for blacks.

Brown's raid began on
October 16, 1859, with 19
African-American and white
men. They cut the telegraph lines
leading to Harpers Ferry,
Virginia, and moved to the
arsenal where military weapons
were stored. Success depended
on hundreds of slaves from
Virginia rising up and joining
the cause. Brown's men took
control of a musket factory, an
armory, a firehouse, and a
railroad station. The men
blocked off the area. They also
arrested prominent slaveholders
in the area, hoping that the slaves
would rebel and help them.

Brown then made the mistake of
releasing the Baltimore-bound train from the station.
Word got out that Harpers Ferry had been invaded; the
Charleston military responded. Brown and his men
took refuge in the engine house and arsenal.

After almost two days of armed fighting, Brown and
a few others were trapped in the arsenal with hostages.

*John Brown's fort at the entrance
of the arsenal at Harpers Ferry*

On October 18, Brown tried to negotiate his way out.
Federal troops led by Robert E. Lee and J.E.B. Stuart
stormed the building. John Brown was captured and
led to jail.

While most commonly known for John Brown's raid, the city of Harpers Ferry is important in America's history for many reasons.

In 1794, at President George Washington's urging, Congress established an armory and arsenal at Harpers Ferry.

In September 1862, during the Civil War, Confederate General "Stonewall" Jackson captured as many as 12,500 Union troops at Harpers Ferry. His men also seized weapons and ammunition from the arsenal.

In 1867, Harpers Ferry opened one of the first integrated schools in the United States to educate former slaves.

On October 25, 1859, Brown and six other men were charged with treason, murder, and plotting to instigate a rebellion. Abolitionists funded Brown's defense, but he was found guilty of treason. On November 2, he was sentenced to hang.

Four days before his execution, Brown wrote,

It is a great comfort to feel assured that I am permitted to die for a cause.[3]

During the rebellion, Tubman was confined to bed. When she learned that Brown's raid had failed, she told of a dream she had just before she met Brown. Tubman dreamed about a serpent in a wilderness full of rocks and bushes. She saw the serpent lift its head and become the head of an old man with a white beard. Two other heads rose beside it, and a crowd of men struck them all down. Tubman realized later that her dream had been about Brown and his two sons. On December 2, 1859, one month after he was sentenced, John Brown was

A scrap of wood from the gallows and a piece of the rope used to hang abolitionist John Brown

hanged. As he approached the gallows, he handed a guard a note:

> I John Brown am now quite certain that the crimes of this guilty land: will never be purged away; but with blood. I had as I now think: vainly flattered myself that without very much bloodshed; it might be done.[4]

Brown's death brought the cause of slavery to the forefront in the minds of Americans. He became the most famous martyr of the abolitionist cause. Writer Henry David Thoreau said,

> *No man in America has ever stood up so persistently and effectively for the dignity of human nature.*[5]

Tubman and many Americans were moved by the cause and the martyrdom of Brown. Tubman vowed to carry on his legacy. ⌐

Harriet Tubman

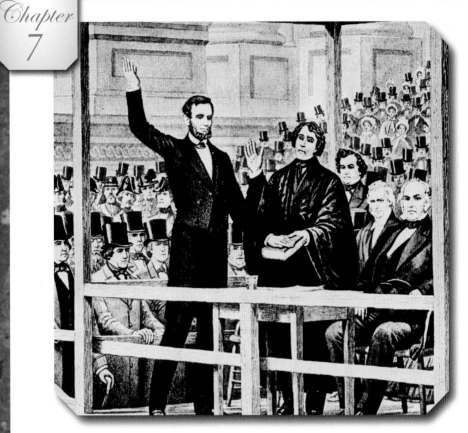

On March 4, 1861, Abraham Lincoln became the sixteenth president of the United States.

CELEBRITY STATUS

ubman's Underground Railroad career began when she was in her twenties. By 1860, she was in her thirties. Abraham Lincoln was elected president of the United States. Tubman was becoming a celebrity among more than Underground Railroad people. She

was asked to speak to raise money for the cause. She
told spellbinding stories of her life and her exploits.
William Wells Brown wrote,

> *The most refined person would listen for hours while she*
> *related the intensely interesting incidents of her life, told in*
> *the simplest manner, but always seasoned with good sense.*[1]

COURTROOM RESCUE

On April 27, 1860, Tubman gained new status as
a fighter when she tried to free Charles Nalle in a
dramatic courtroom rescue. Nalle, a black coachman,
had escaped slavery in 1858. While living in the North,
he was caught and was to be returned to his master in
the South. The slave catcher, a free black, was Nalle's
brother.

Nalle was being held at the Mutual Bank Building in
Troy, New York. Tubman had stopped in the town
on her way to a speaking engagement in Boston. As
Nalle's hearing was about to begin at the courthouse,
antislavery protestors gathered outside. Pro-slavery
supporters had gathered too. The crowd was large. Ever
the planner, Tubman had arranged for a boat to be
waiting at the riverbank in case she should need it.

Dressed as an old woman, Tubman wore a

sunbonnet and carried a food basket. Bent over and seeming very weak and frail, she was let into the courtroom, although most people were not allowed inside. She was in the back of the room when the decision was announced to send Nalle back to his master in Virginia.

In an effort to escape, Nalle managed to climb out a window. He was hauled back in, and his hands and feet were bound. Tubman, as the old woman, went into action. She threw off her shawl, grabbed Nalle, and dragged him downstairs to the crowd. Tubman was beaten on the head, but she did not let go of Nalle. The crowd rallied around Tubman and carried Nalle to the boat waiting at the riverbank.

Douglass and Tubman

The great abolitionist Frederick Douglass once said of Harriet Tubman:

"*The difference between us is very marked. Most that I have done and suffered in the service of our cause has been in public, and I have received encouragement at every step of the way. You, on the other hand, have labored in a private way. I have wrought in the day—you at night. I have had the applause of the crowd and the satisfaction that comes of being approved by the multitude, while the most that you have done has been witnessed by a few trembling, scared and footsore bondsmen and women, whom you have led out of the house of bondage, and whose heartfelt God bless you has been your only reward. The midnight sky and the silent stars have been the witnesses of your devotion to freedom and of your heroism.*"[2]

However, when the boat reached the other side of the river, Nalle was arrested and returned to the courthouse.

Nalle was taken to a judge's office until he could be safely transported south. However, the angry crowd followed. At Tubman's signal, the crowd rallied and stormed the judge's office. A huge black man was at the front of the crowd. He pulled open the judge's door, but the deputy sheriff hit him over the head. The man's large body crumpled to the floor and served to hold the door open.

Tubman and others rushed over his body and dragged Nalle out of the judge's office. A man was driving by in a horse and buggy. He was asked to stop. He did, and Nalle was put inside the buggy, which immediately headed out of town.

Although others died in the attempt, Nalle was taken to safety in Canada. The story, of course, was big news. Tubman had gained new status as a freedom fighter.

A WANTED WOMAN

A bounty (or reward) was offered for her capture. Now officials were looking for the little old lady in the sunbonnet. Rewards varied from $12,000 to $40,000; if she were caught, she would be executed.

Rewards for Tubman's capture did not immediately slow her down. She was confident that she would live to see slaves emancipated. The bounty on her head was not going to keep her in hiding. In May of 1860, Tubman continued on to Boston, Massachusetts, to speak at the New England Anti-Slavery Society Conference. She agreed to speak under a pseudonym, however, because of the reward for her capture.

In December 1860, Tubman set off to rescue a couple and their two children from Maryland. She guided the family safely to Canada, but it was becoming too dangerous for her to return to the South. She had become too well known, and the bounty had become too high. There was no way of knowing how many slave catchers were hunting her. This was Tubman's last rescue mission for the Underground Railroad, but she was far from finished freeing slaves.

The War Between the States (the Civil War) was about to begin, and Tubman was not going to miss out on the opportunity to free all the slaves in the South. She returned to the United States. Not concerned about her newfound celebrity status, she was ready for a good fight.

A sculpture of Harriet Tubman honors her role in leading slaves to freedom.

Union troops recapturing artillery at Shiloh, Tennessee, in 1862

THE CIVIL WAR

In February of 1861, Jefferson Davis became president of the Confederate States of America. The southern half of the country was pulling away from the United States of America. On April 12, 1861, the Confederates fired on Fort Sumter in South

Carolina. Soon after, President Lincoln blockaded southern ports and requested volunteers to help put down the rebellion. Lincoln's goal was to preserve the Union.

At the beginning of the Civil War, President Lincoln did not intend to free the slaves. Even though black troops rallied in Pittsburgh, Cleveland, Boston, and other cities, Lincoln prohibited blacks from enlisting in the army.

Massachusetts Governor John Andrew was an abolitionist, and he asked Tubman to join his state volunteers. The plan was to use black scouts and spies to infiltrate the South and collect information. More importantly, many slaves feared the Yankees more than they feared their masters. Once the Union Army freed them, the slaves would need people they trusted to help them adjust to life as free people.

Tubman was excited by the prospect. She was certain that a Union victory would mean the end of slavery. In May 1861, she informally attached herself to the

Preliminary Proclamation

President Lincoln's Preliminary Emancipation Proclamation, which he issued September 22, 1862, states in part:

"... on the first day of January ... all persons held as slaves within any state, or designated part of a state, the people whereof shall be then, thenceforward, and forever free."[1]

Massachusetts troops. The New England Freedman's Aid Society sponsored her. She was taken south on a federal ship, the *Atlantic*, to join General Benjamin Butler's men at Fort Monroe on the western shore of the Chesapeake Bay in Maryland. Fort Monroe was surrounded by water on three sides. Butler offered protection to runaway slaves by claiming that they were contraband of war.

Fort Monroe became a place to which slaves escaped. Within three months, more than 1,000 escaped slaves found refuge at Fort Monroe. Less than one year later, the number reached 3,000.

Tubman was helping the slaves find escape routes and Union sanctuary. She talked to the refugees about working to help the Union Army fight for their freedom.

The Emancipation Proclamation

The Emancipation Proclamation was issued January 1, 1863. In part, it read:

"... I, Abraham Lincoln, President of the United States, ... do order and declare that all persons held as slaves within said designated States, and parts of States, are, and henceforward shall be free ... And I hereby enjoin upon the people so declared to be free to abstain from all violence, unless in necessary self-defence ... they labor faithfully for reasonable wages. And I further declare and make known, that such persons of suitable condition, will be received into the armed service of the United States. ... And upon this act, sincerely believed to be an act of justice, warranted by the Constitution ... I invoke the considerate judgment of mankind. ..."[2]

She helped the refugees deal with their new lives. Now they had choices. Because they were not allowed to fight, many of the refugees picked cotton on abandoned plantations for the Union Army. The women cooked and washed for the Union Army.

On November 7, 1861, Tubman was visiting New England when she heard of the Union's capture of Port Royal, South Carolina. President Lincoln had set up a naval blockade of that important Confederate port. In May 1862, Tubman journeyed to the South Carolina seacoast. She had been drafted to work with Dr. Henry K. Durant at the Freedman's Hospital in Port Royal. The soldiers at the hospital soon learned that they were working with the famed Moses.

Tubman was not paid for her work. At first, she collected government food for herself. When she realized there was not enough food for all the refugees, she gave it up. Instead, after a day's work was done, she made root beer and pies to sell to the men in the Union Army. She worked for free and earned money for her food.

Root Doctor

Three out of five Civil War soldiers died. They often died from diseases not related to their wounds. In Port Royal, Tubman worked as a nurse and root doctor. As a young girl, she had learned which plants that grew in the wild could cure illnesses. Now, she collected plants to make medicine. Her fame as a root doctor grew.

Although Tubman was working hard for the Union Army, she was reluctant to support President Lincoln because ending slavery was not his goal. Finally, in July 1862, President Lincoln did decide to work toward freeing slaves. And on September 22, he issued his Preliminary Emancipation Proclamation. It said that as of January 1, 1863, all slaves in areas still in rebellion would be declared free. Lincoln's intention was to defeat the rebels by pressuring slaveholders to urge their states to rejoin the Union. It did not work. The slaveholders did not try to get their states to rejoin the Union. But Lincoln's Preliminary Emancipation Proclamation did broaden the Union cause. The Civil War became a war to free the slaves.

Tubman was pleased with the president's decision. Her service in the army was about to change. She continued serving as a scout, spy, nurse, and root doctor. But she did more than that. Harriet Tubman became the first woman in American history to lead troops into battle.

In pursuance of the sixth section of the act of congress entitled "An act to suppress insurrection and to punish treason and rebellion, to seize and confiscate property of rebels, and for other purposes" Approved July 17. 1862, and which act, and the Joint Resolution explanatory thereof, are herewith published, I, Abraham Lincoln, President of the United States, do hereby proclaim to, and warn all persons within the contemplation of said sixth section to cease participating in, aiding, countenancing, or abetting the existing rebellion, or any rebellion against the government of the United States, and to return to their proper allegiance to the United States, on pain of the forfeitures and seizures, as within and by said sixth section provided—

And I hereby make known that it is my purpose, upon the next meeting of Congress, to again recommend the adoption of a practical measure for tendering pecuniary aid to the free choice or rejection, of any and all States which may then be recognizing and practically sustaining the authority of the United States, and which may then have voluntarily adopted, or thereafter may voluntarily adopt, gradual abolishment ~~adoption~~ of slavery within such State or States— that the object is to practically restore, thenceforward to maintain, the constitutional relation between the general government, and each, and all the States, wherein that relation

A first draft of President Lincoln's Emancipation Proclamation

The Battle of Gettysburg, July 1863

FIGHTING FOR FREEDOM

*I*n 1863, after ten months nursing the sick, Tubman was given the authority to gather a group of scouts to work their way inland, map the area, and collect information. Her group became an official scouting service under the direction of Secretary of

State Edwin M. Stanton. She provided military intelligence to Union Colonel James Montgomery. This resulted in successful raids on many coastal Confederate towns.

On June 2, 1863, Tubman led a battalion of blacks—the Second Carolina Volunteers—in the Combahee River Raid. Three federal ships went up St. Helena Sound carrying Colonel Montgomery, Tubman, and approximately 150 black soldiers. Fugitive slaves hid along the shores. This was a sneak attack in the dead of night. The Confederates were taken by surprise. When the Union troops went ashore, they destroyed Confederate crops, barns, houses, and plantations. They also brought more than 750 slaves onto the armed Union ship.

The Combahee River Raid created an opportunity for the Union Army to help the refugees. Former slaves could now join the Union Army knowing that their families were safe from the Confederacy and from their former masters.

Dressing for Expeditions

After the raid, Tubman not only helped the refugees board the ship, she also helped a woman get her two pigs onto one of the ships. Tubman stepped on the hem of her dress, trying to wrestle the pigs onto the ship. She declared she would never wear a skirt on a military expedition again.

Later, she dictated a letter to the ladies of Boston so that they would be aware of her wardrobe problems. Tubman stated, "I want ... a bloomer dress, made of some coarse, strong material, to wear on expeditions."[1]

Tubman's heroism was praised—in an offhanded manner. The front page of the *Boston Commonwealth* read like a tall tale with larger-than-life figures.

> *Colonel Montgomery and his gallant band of 300 black soldiers, under the guidance of a black woman, dashed into the enemies' country, struck a bold and effective blow, destroying millions of dollars worth of commissary stores, cotton and lordly dwellings, and striking terror to the heart of rebel-dom, brought off near 800 slaves and thousands of dollars worth of property, without losing a man or receiving a scratch!*[2]

Tubman told the story in her own words:

The Gettysburg Address

President Lincoln delivered the Gettysburg Address on November 19, 1863, as he dedicated the Soldier's National Cemetery at Gettysburg, Pennsylvania.

"*Four score and seven years ago our fathers brought forth on this continent, a new nation, conceived in Liberty, and dedicated to the proposition that all men are created equal.*

Now we are engaged in a great civil war ... We are met on a great battle field of that war. We have come to dedicate a portion of that field, as a final resting place for those who here gave their lives that the nation might live. It is altogether fitting and proper that we should do this...

The world will little note, nor long remember what we say here, but it can never forget what they did here... that these dead shall not have died in vain—that this nation, under God, shall have a new birth of freedom—and that government of the people, by the people, for the people, shall not perish from the earth."[3]

President Lincoln giving the Gettysburg Address in 1863 during the Civil War

We weakened the rebels somewhat in the Combahee River by taking and bringing away seven hundred and fifty six head of their most valuable live stock, known up in your region as "contrabands," and this, too, without the loss of a single life on our part, though we had good reason to believe that a number of rebels bit the dust.[4]

Clara Barton

Clara Barton was a nurse and a philanthropist who worked to improve human welfare. She worked for a short time during the Civil War as superintendent of nurses under the command of Major General Benjamin F. Butler. Barton founded the American Red Cross in 1881.

The Thirteenth Amendment

The Thirteenth Amendment to the U.S. Constitution was ratified in December of 1865:

"Neither slavery nor involuntary servitude, except as a punishment for crime whereof the party shall have been duly convicted, shall exist within the United States, or any place subject to their jurisdiction."[5]

This boast was unusual. By necessity, Tubman had always been very secretive about her dealings.

Tubman's name was not in any military records. She seemed to be invisible, both to the enemy troops and to the officials under whom she served. Often in newspaper accounts, if she was mentioned at all, she was mentioned only as "a black woman." Much of what is written about her war work was written later, when she applied for a pension from the army.

From January to April 1863, approximately 1,000 black soldiers prepared for combat. The black regiment, the Massachusetts' Fifty-fourth, was involved in the assault on Fort Wagner on July 18.

The Confederates held their own, and by July 19, it was clear that it had been a particularly bloody battle. The Massachusetts Fifty-fourth lost 272 soldiers. Of the 5,000 Union men fighting at Fort Wagner, more than 1,500 were killed, wounded, or captured.

Tubman spent the rest of the summer nursing the men from the Massachusetts Fifty-fourth Regiment and other African-American Union soldiers. During the fall of 1863, her health was not good, but she continued working through the winter. Finally, in May 1864, she requested leave to go home.

Her commanding officers, General Rufus Saxton and surgeon Henry Durant, commended her service and signed a certificate for her to take military transportation from South Carolina to New York. Tubman went home to Auburn, New York, to see her parents.

By 1864, Tubman was suffering more frequent spells from the skull fracture. At times, she would fall asleep in the middle of a sentence. While in Boston, she had surgery. It helped somewhat, but the symptoms did not disappear. Still, Tubman headed back to work.

In January 1865, the Thirteenth Amendment, abolishing slavery, was proposed. It was ratified in December 1865, having been passed by most of the states. Only Mississippi did not ratify it.

In March 1865, Tubman traveled to Washington, D.C., to obtain permission for military transport back to South Carolina. On her journey, she stopped in Philadelphia and was requested to work in the Virginia hospital wards. Tubman headed for Virginia.

On April 2, 1865, the Confederates evacuated their capital, Richmond, Virginia. On April 9, General

Robert E. Lee surrendered the Confederate Army to Union General Ulysses S. Grant at the courthouse in Appomattox, Virginia. The war had ended. On April 14, President Lincoln was assassinated in Ford's Theater and died on April 15. The war-torn country mourned.

Tubman continued to work in Virginia through June of 1865. Supplies were limited, and the conditions were horrible. Tubman decided she must go to Washington, D.C., to solicit help. In the nation's capital, she made an appeal for supplies and better conditions. While there, she was appointed Nurse (or Matron). Tubman was the first African-American woman to be granted that particular honor.

She returned to Virginia on July 22, 1865, but still had no supplies. As she had not received regular salary or back pay, she had no way to take care of her own needs. She did what she could for the men who remained in the hospital then headed home.

The Cost of Human Lives

Prior to the Civil War, most medical doctors in the United States did not go to school. They learned as apprentices. They did not know much about disease and infection. They did not know to sterilize their equipment. Surgeons might go days without washing

John Wilkes Booth shot President Abraham Lincoln in Ford's Theater in 1865.

their hands or surgical tools. At the beginning of the Civil War, the Union Army had 98 medical officers, and the Confederate Army had 24. By 1865, about 13,000 doctors had served the Union Army and about 4,000 doctors had served the Confederate Army. Thousands of women donated their time to work as nurses. Approximately 620,000 men from both sides died in the war. About 200,000 of those men died from battle wounds. The rest died of diseases such as typhoid fever, dysentery, pneumonia, and malaria. Army camps were filthy, which added to the high rate of death.

THE ROAD HOME AND NEW BATTLES

On her way home from the war, Tubman traveled by train. In New Jersey, a conductor believed that her traveling papers were forged. He asked her to leave her seat, but she refused. It took four men to pull Tubman out of her seat. They beat her and dumped her in the baggage car, where she rode the rest of the way to Auburn, New York. Her injuries took months to heal.

Now that the war was over and the slaves were freed, the next struggle for blacks was the right to vote. Frederick Douglass said it well:

> If he knows enough to take up arms in defense of this government and bare his breast to the storm of rebel artillery, he knows enough to vote.[6]

Harriet Tubman spent her remaining years fighting for the legal status, dignity, and rights of women and African Americans. ⌐

Celebration of the abolition of slavery in Washington, D.C., 1866

The statue "Step on Board" of Harriet Tubman

GOOD DEEDS

After the war, Harriet Tubman returned to Auburn, New York, to live with her family, friends, and the needy people who were staying in her small house. Her small home was always open to people who needed shelter. In about 1866 or 1867,

Tubman met a young black soldier named Private Nelson Charles. He also used the name Charles Nelson Davis. Born a slave in North Carolina, he had escaped his master and moved to upstate New York. In September 1863, he joined the New York Eighth Regiment, Company G. He trained in Philadelphia, then the regiment moved south in January 1864.

It is possible that Private Charles and Tubman may have met in the South during the war. He fought in a few battles and was honorably discharged from the Union Army in November 1865. He arrived in Auburn the following winter. Private Charles moved into Tubman's home to recuperate from tuberculosis.

In 1867, John Tubman, Harriet's husband who had refused to go north with her, was killed in Dorchester County, Maryland. Harriet Tubman was free to remarry if she chose. On March 18, 1869, she married Charles Nelson Davis at Auburn's Central Presbyterian Church. Davis was 25 years old, and Tubman was in her forties.

Women's Rights

Harriet Tubman attended women's rights gatherings in upstate New York as long as she was able to. On October 23, 1905, she went to a meeting in Rochester. After she arrived by train in town, she sat all night in the train station because there was no lodging in town for blacks. She never complained, but her white friends made sure that she had appropriate lodging from then on.

GETTING BY

Tubman had almost no income. Now that she was married and responsible for so many people in her home, she could not travel to find work. Her friends sponsored an authorized biography, drafted by Sarah Bradford. *Scenes in the Life of Harriet Tubman* consisted of stories told by Tubman and some of her abolitionist friends. Published in 1869, Tubman received $1,200.

Friends helped her petition the government for a soldier's pension. Tubman had received only $200 in pay during her years in the service. She used the money to build a laundry to teach freed women how to support themselves by doing laundry.

In 1886, Tubman's home was destroyed by fire. She rebuilt. Tubman knew it was important to keep her home open because few of the homes for the aged in the area admitted blacks. She had a dream of building a charity home for aged and ill black people.

By the late 1880s, the money from

A Family Memory

Tubman's niece and adopted daughter, Margaret, had grown up, married, and had children. She would often bring her children to Tubman's house for visits and stories.

Margaret's daughter, Alice, told of a time when she was playing in the long grass, and Grandmother Harriet suddenly popped up beside her. Grandmother Harriet had left her rocking chair on the porch and gotten down in the grass and slithered along—a trick she had learned in the Underground Railroad.

Title page for Scenes in the Life of Harriet Tubman

the 1869 book about her life was gone, and Tubman
had no reliable income. Sarah Bradford published
Harriet, the Moses of Her People. The good ladies of Auburn
took turns leaving baskets of food on Tubman's
doorstep.

An Activist

Tubman became a speaker for women's right to vote. When asked by a white woman if she thought women should have the vote, Tubman's response was "I suffered enough to believe it."[1]

In October 1888, Charles Nelson Davis passed away. He was buried at Fort Hill Cemetery. Tubman and Davis had been married for nearly 20 years. Two years after his death, Tubman applied for a pension for widows of war veterans. She had to document everything to receive the pension. On the application, she swore that she was born in 1825. Her husband's name had changed, so she had to verify

Tributes

Over the past 100 years, Harriet Tubman has been remembered in many ways. Schools, libraries, and other civic establishments have been named in her honor. A few of the very special tributes include:

- In 1914, the citizens of Auburn, New York, honored Tubman with a memorial plaque. The inscription describes Tubman as "... the Moses of her people, during the Civil War. With rare courage, she led over three hundred negroes up from slavery to freedom and rendered invaluable service as nurse and spy."
- In 1944, Eleanor Roosevelt christened a U.S. Liberty ship the USS *Harriet Tubman*.
- In 1977, the U.S. Postal Service issued a stamp in honor of Harriet Tubman. The stamp commemorated Black History Week.
- Harriet Tubman was one of the first women to be included in the National Women's Hall of Fame in Seneca Falls, New York, the site of the first women's rights convention in America. It was established in 1968.

that he was the same person who had served in the
Union Army. At the end of 1892, more than two
years after she had applied, and four years after her
husband's death, Tubman finally was granted a widow's
pension of $8 a month. She had not received a pension
for her own work in the army; she only received a
pension as the widow of a soldier.

Tubman was almost 70, and for the first time in
her life, she had a steady income. She could not rest,
though. She wanted to construct a building to house
needy black people. In 1896, Tubman attended a local
public auction and outbid everyone for a property
near her house. Her bid for the property was $1,450,
but she did not have the money to pay for it. Tubman
did the same thing that she had done for the
Underground Railroad—she asked others to help her
come up with the money for a good cause.

Tubman was a senior founder of the National
Association of Colored Women. It was formed by a
merger of several organizations at a convention in
Washington, D.C., in July 1896. The association still
exists to support the rights of African-American
women.

In 1897, a petition was made for Tubman to receive
a soldier's pension for her war service. She had never

The Harriet Tubman Home in Auburn, New York

been compensated for her time helping the Union
Army. The regular soldier's pension was $25 a month,
the amount all retired soldiers received. It was finally
decided to raise her widow's pension from $8 a month
to $20 a month, due to "special circumstances."
Tubman began receiving her new pension in February
1899. To receive her soldier's pension, she had to
describe details of her wartime service. Because
Tubman had been an "unofficial" spy, scout, nurse,

and root doctor for the Union Army, no records had been kept. With this retelling, Tubman's Union Army service became part of the Congressional Record.

Also in 1897, the New England Women's Suffrage Association honored Harriet Tubman for her dedication to freedom. In 1904, Susan B. Anthony introduced her as a living legend at the 28th Annual Convention of the New York State Women's Suffrage Association.

The Harriet Tubman Home

In 1903, Tubman donated the property she had bought a few years earlier to her church, the African Methodist Episcopal Zion Church. In her eighties, the upkeep of the property and the money needed for repairs became too much for her. She made it clear to her church that she expected to see a shelter built on the property. On June 23, 1908, the Harriet Tubman Home was established in Auburn, New York. The church charged $3 a week or $150 for a lifetime of care at the home. Tubman thought it was an outrage that poor, homeless, sick people had to pay a church. She did what she could; she continued to knock on doors to solicit funds for people to stay there. She also continued to solicit funds for freedmen's schools and the Salvation Army, as well as for her church. Sarah Bradford described Tubman's relentless generosity:

> *Her household is very likely to consist of several old black people … How she manages to feed and clothe herself and them, the Lord best knows. She has too much pride and too much faith to beg. She takes thankfully … whatever God's messengers bring her.*

> *Harriet's simplicity and ignorance have, in some cases, been imposed upon … but nobody who knows her has the slightest doubt of her perfect integrity.*[2]

Her health failing, in 1911 Tubman moved into the Harriet Tubman Home, next door to her house. She prepared a will in 1912, leaving everything to her nieces and the matron of her charity home. On March 10, 1913, Harriet died of pneumonia at the home. She was given a military funeral and buried in Fort Hill Cemetery in Auburn, forever a true soldier in the cause of freedom. ⌐

Harriet Tubman at home in Auburn, New York, 1911

TIMELINE

1820?	1831	1844
Araminta "Minty" Ross is born into slavery. The exact year is unknown.	Nat Turner's rebellion.	Harriet marries John Tubman.

1857	1858	1860
Tubman rescues her parents who were in danger from harboring fugitive slaves.	Tubman meets the abolitionist John Brown.	Tubman gains new status as she fights to free Charles Nalle on April 27.

1849	1850	1852
Harriet Tubman escapes to Philadelphia.	Fugitive Slave Law; Tubman makes her first rescue of relatives.	Harriet Beecher Stowe's *Uncle Tom's Cabin* is published.

1860	1861	1863
Tubman makes her last rescue with the Underground Railroad in December.	Tubman volunteers to help the Union Army in the Civil War.	The Emancipation Proclamation freed slaves in the South on January 1.

TIMELINE

1863	1865	1869
Tubman leads the Combahee River Raid on June 2.	Tubman returns to Auburn at the end of the Civil War.	Tubman marries Charles Nelson Davis on March 18.

1888	1896
Tubman's husband, Charles Nelson Davis, dies.	Tubman buys property for a future home for aged and indigent black people.

1869

Sarah Bradford writes
*Scenes in the Life of Harriet
Tubman.*

1886

Sarah Bradford writes
*Harriet, The Moses
of Her People.*

1908

The Harriet Tubman
Home opens on June 23.

1913

Tubman dies on March 10.

ESSENTIAL FACTS

Date of Birth
No official record; most likely born between 1820-1825 and named
Harriet Araminta Ross.

Place of Birth
No official record; most likely born on the Brodess plantation in
Maryland.

Date of Death
March 10, 1913

Place of Death
The Harriet Tubman Home in Auburn, New York

Parents
Harriet "Rit" Green and Ben Ross

Education
None; illiterate

Marriage
1844 to John Tubman; March 18, 1869, to Charles Nelson Davis

Children
Adopted her niece Margaret.

Career Highlights
Eight years as an Underground Railroad conductor; worked with the Massachusetts troops in the Civil War as a scout and spy; a nurse in the Civil War; the first woman in American history to lead troops into battle.

Societal Contribution
Fought for the legal status and rights of women and African Americans; founded a shelter for poor, homeless, and sick African Americans.

Residencies
Brodess plantation in Maryland; Philadelphia, Pennsylvania; St. Catherines in Ontario, Canada; Auburn, New York.

Travels
Apart from her trips bringing slaves to freedom, Tubman's travels included trips to Massachusetts and New York in support of abolition and women's suffrage rights.

Conflicts
While Tubman worked for the Union Army, she was reluctant to support President Lincoln because ending slavery was not his goal. Not until 1863, with Lincoln's Emancipation Proclamation, did the Civil War become a war to free the slaves.

Quote
"But to this solemn resolution I came: I was free and they should be free also...."—Harriet Tubman

ADDITIONAL RESOURCES

SELECT BIBLIOGRAPHY

Alexander, Amy. *Fifty Black Women Who Changed America*. Secaucus, NJ: n.p., 1999.

Bordewich, Fergus M. *Bound for Canaan: The Underground Railroad and the War for the Soul of America*. New York: HarperCollins, 2005.

Bradford, Sarah H. *Harriet, the Moses of Her People*. New York: n.p., 1886. Project Gutenberg, 2006.

Carrasco, Hazel, and Owen Solberg. *Underground Railroad: The Fugitive Slave Bill of 1850*. <http://www.education.ucdavis.edu/NEW/STC/lesson/ socstud/railroad/SlaveLaw.html>.

Clinton, Catherine. *Harriet Tubman: The Road to Freedom*. New York: Little, Brown, and Company, 2004.

Cullen-DuPont, Kathryn. *The Encyclopedia of Women's History in America*. New York: Facts On File, Inc., 1996.

King, John T., and Marcet H. King. *Famous Negro Americans*. Austin, Texas: Steck-Vaughn, 1967.

Marlow, Joan. *The Great Women*. New York: A & W Publishers, Inc. 1979.

FURTHER READING

Clinton, Catherine. *Harriet Tubman: The Road to Freedom*. New York: Little, Brown, and Company, 2004.

Humez, Jean M. *Harriet Tubman: The Life and the Life Stories (Wisconsin Studies in Autobiography)*. Madison, WI: University of Wisconsin Press, 2004.

McClard, Megan. *Harriet Tubman: Slavery and the Underground Railroad*. Englewood Cliffs, NJ: Silver Burdett Press, 1991.

Web Links

To learn more about Harriet Tubman, visit ABDO Publishing Company on the World Wide Web at **www.abdopublishing.com.** Web sites about Harriet Tubman are featured on our Book Links page. These links are routinely monitored and updated to provide the most current information available.

Places to Visit

The Harriet Tubman Home for the Aged
180 South Street, Auburn, NY 13201
315-252-2081
www.nyhistory.com/harriettubman/
Tubman bought the property in 1896. In 1908 she donated it to the African Methodist Episcopal Zion church as a shelter for African-Americans.

The Civil War and Underground Railroad Museum of Philadelphia
South 18th Street and Pine Street, Philadelphia, PA 19103
215-735-8196
www.cwurmuseum.org
This museum displays items of the Civil War period and exhibits related to the experiences of women and black soldiers of the time.

Ford's Theater
511 10th Street, Washington, D.C. 20004
202-426-6924
www.nps.gov/archive/foth/index2.htm
Visit the theater in which President Lincoln was assassinated. See the clothes he wore and the flag that covered his coffin.

Glossary

abolitionists
People who worked to abolish slavery before the Civil War.

anonymity
The state of not being known or identified by name.

armory
A building in which weapons are stored.

bondage
The condition of being a slave.

bounty hunter
A person who pursues another for a reward.

commitment
Devoted to a cause.

commotion
Noisy confusion.

contraband
Illegal goods.

emancipate
To free someone from slavery.

fracture
A break or crack in a bone.

fugitive
A person who flees from danger or justice.

illiterate
Uneducated; unable to read and write.

indigent
> Poor or needy.

insurrection
> Rebellion against a government or authority.

negotiate
> Bargain or discuss to reach an agreement.

preserve
> To keep safe from destruction.

pseudonym
> False name.

refugee
> A person seeking shelter or a safe place.

sanctuary
> A safe place.

status
> Position or standing in society.

suffrage
> The right to vote in a public election.

supplement
> To make an addition to.

treason
> Violation of allegiance to one's country.

Source Notes

Chapter 1. A Hit on the Head

1. Sarah H. Bradford. *Harriet, the Moses of Her People.* New York: n.p., 1886. Project Gutenberg, 2006. N. pag.

Chapter 2. Growing Up as a Slave

1. Fergus M. Bordewich. *Bound for Canaan: The Underground Railroad and the War for the Soul of America.* New York: HarperCollins, 2005. 347.

Chapter 3. A Taste of Freedom

1. Catherine Clinton. *Harriet Tubman: The Road to Freedom.* New York: Little, Brown, and Company, 2004. 32.

2. Ibid. 34.

3. Sarah H. Bradford. *Harriet, the Moses of Her People.* New York: n.p., 1886. Project Gutenberg, 2006. N. pag.

4. Ibid.

5. Hazel Carrascso and Owen Solberg. *Underground Railroad: The Fugitive Slave Bill of 1850.* <http://education.ucdavis.edu/NEW/STC/lesson/socstud/railroad/SlaveLaw.html>.

6. "Harriet Tubman." *The Underground Railroad History Living Experience.* Civil War & Underground Railroad Museum of Philadelphia. 14 May 2007 <http://www.magpi.net/programs/documents/Harriet%20Tubman%20Living%20History%20Experience.pdf>.

Chapter 4. The Underground Railroad

1. Sojurner Truth. "Ain't I a Woman." *Modern History Sourcebook.* Aug. 1977. Fordham University. 11 Nov. 2006 <http://www.fordham.edu/halsell/mod/sojtruth-woman.html>.

2. Catherine Clinton. *Harriet Tubman: The Road to Freedom.* New York: Little, Brown, and Company, 2004. 221.

3. Ibid. 192.

Chapter 5. Together and Free!

1. Catherine Clinton. *Harriet Tubman: The Road to Freedom.* New York: Little, Brown, and Company, 2004. 84.

2. Fergus M. Bordewich. *Bound for Canaan: The Underground Railroad and the War for the Soul of America.* New York: HarperCollins, 2005. 352.

3. Catherine Clinton. *Harriet Tubman: The Road to Freedom.* New York: Little, Brown, and Company, 2004. 77.

4. Fergus M. Bordewich. *Bound for Canaan: The Underground Railroad and the War for the Soul of America.* New York: HarperCollins, 2005. 374.

Chapter 6. Not Afraid of Danger

1. Catherine Clinton. *Harriet Tubman: The Road to Freedom.* New York: Little, Brown, and Company, 2004. 92.

2. Fergus M. Bordewich. *Bound for Canaan: The Underground Railroad and the War for the Soul of America.* New York: HarperCollins, 2005. 352.

3. Catherine Clinton. *Harriet Tubman: The Road to Freedom.* New York: Little, Brown, and Company, 2004. 135.

4. Fergus M. Bordewich. *Bound for Canaan: The Underground Railroad and the War for the Soul of America.* New York: HarperCollins, 2005. 426.

5. *Judgment Day, Part 4: 1831–1865.* PBS Online. 15 May 2007 <http://www.pbs.org/wgbh/aia/part4/4p1550.html>.

Chapter 7. Celebrity Status

1. Catherine Clinton. *Harriet Tubman: The Road to Freedom.* New York: Little, Brown, and Company, 2004. 87.

2. Joan Marlow. *The Great Women.* New York: A & W Publishers, Inc. 1979. 73.

Chapter 8. The Civil War

1. Abraham Lincoln. "Lincoln's Preliminary Emancipation Proclamation." *The Emancipation Proclamation.* 24 Nov. 2006. New York State Library. 15 May 2007 <http://nysl.nysed.gov.library/features/ep/#hans>.

SOURCE NOTES CONTINUED

2. Abraham Lincoln. "The Emancipation Proclamation." U.S. National Archives & Records Administration. 15 May 2007 <http://www/archives.gov/exhibits/featured_documents/emancipation_proclamation/transcript.html>.

Chapter 9. Fighting for Freedom

1. Kathryn Cullen-DuPont. *The Encyclopedia of Women's History in America*. New York: Facts On File, Inc., 1996. 58.

2. Ibid. 211.

3. Roy B. Basler, ed. *The Collected Works of Abraham Lincoln*, vol. 7 (1953-1955). 22. <http://www.loc.gov/exhibits/gadd/gainvi.html>.

4. Catherine Clinton. *Harriet Tubman: The Road to Freedom*. New York: Little, Brown, and Company, 2004. 173.

5. Steve Mount. "United States Constitution." *The U.S. Constitution Online*, 6 Mar. 2007. <http://www.usconstitution.net/const.html#Am13>.

6. Catherine Clinton. *Harriet Tubman: The Road to Freedom*. New York: Little, Brown, and Company, 2004. 187.

Chapter 10. Good Deeds

1. Catherine Clinton. *Harriet Tubman: The Road to Freedom*. New York: Little, Brown, and Company, 2004. 191.

2. Samuel Miles Hopkins, Jr. Introduction. *Harriet the Moses of Her People*. By Sarah H. Bradford. New York: n.p., 1886. Project Guttenberg, 2006. N. pag.

INDEX

Index Continued

ABOUT THE AUTHOR

M. J. Cosson has held several supervisory positions in publishing, hiring, and managing all types of employees. She currently writes fiction and nonfiction books for children and young adults.

PHOTO CREDITS

Library of Congress/AP Photo, Cover, 3, 63, 96 (top); North Wind Picture Archives, 6, 14, 19, 20, 23, 32, 36, 43, 47, 55, 70, 75, 76, 83, 85, 96 (bottom), 97; Lindaanne Donohoe, 11; AP Photo, 12, 25, 29, 56, 58-59, 64, 79, 92, 98 ; Wilton Historical Society, Douglas Healey/AP Photo, 31; Susan B. Anthony House/AP Photo, 39; Bettmann/Corbis, 40; Wilton Historical Society/AP Photo, 44; David Duprey/AP Photo, 49; Louie Psihoyos/Corbis, 51; Theowulf Maehl/zefa/Corbis, 52; Daily Record, Paul Kuehnel/AP Photo, 61; Carlos Osorio/AP Photo, 69; Gail Oskin/AP Photo, 86; Courtesy University of North Carolina at Chapel Hill Libraries, 89, 99 (top); Library of Congress, 95, 99 (bottom)